Volcanoes

Laaren Brown

SCHOLASTIC INC.
New York   Toronto   London   Auckland
Sydney   Mexico City   New Delhi   Hong Kong

Read more! Do more!

Download your free all-new digital book,
Volcanoes Reading Fun

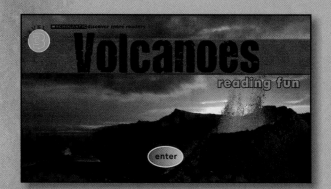

Quizzes to test your knowledge and reading skills

Fun activities to share what you've discovered

Log on to
www.scholastic.com/discovermore/readers
Enter this special code: L3DMX4247MP3

Contents

Copyright © 2013 by Scholastic Inc.

All rights reserved. Published by Scholastic Inc., *Publishers since 1920.*
SCHOLASTIC, SCHOLASTIC DISCOVER MORE™, and associated logos are trademarks and/or registered trademarks of Scholastic Inc.

No part of this publication may be reproduced, stored in a retrieval system, or transmitted in any form or by any means, electronic, mechanical, photocopying, recording, or otherwise, without written permission of the publisher.
For information regarding permission, write to Scholastic Inc., Attention: Permissions Department, 557 Broadway, New York, NY 10012.

ISBN (Trade) 978-0-545-53378-2
ISBN (Clubs) 978-0-545-62413-8

12 11 10 9 8 7 6 5 4 3 2 1   13 14 15 16 17 18/0

Printed in the U.S.A. 40
This edition first printing, August 2013

Scholastic is constantly working to lessen the environmental impact of our manufacturing processes. To view our industry-leading paper procurement policy, visit www.scholastic.com/paperpolicy.

Your world is erupting

Right now, at least ten volcanoes are blowing their tops. People may be in danger. They could be killed by gas and ash. There could be mudflows or red-hot lava flows. An erupting volcano can mean death.

But rock and ash from long-ago volcanoes helped form our beautiful planet.

HOT FACT!

About 80 percent of Earth's volcani

Today, scientists who study volcanoes can help us learn to live with these awesome forces of nature.

eruptions happen under the oceans.

How volcanoes work

Earth isn't really a big solid ball. Its surface is like a 3-D jigsaw puzzle. Enormous puzzle pieces, called plates, fit tightly together. At the edges of the plates, heat and pressure melt the rock that lies deep inside Earth. The melted rock is called magma.

Plates pull apart, and magma rises to fill the gap............

Plate

Types of lava flow

Some types of lava flow have cool names. *Aa* means "rough." *Pahoehoe* means "smooth." Comfy-looking pillow lava forms only underwater.

Aa

Pahoehoe

Magma is always trying to rise up. It may find a crack or vent in Earth's surface and burst out as lava. That's an eruption!

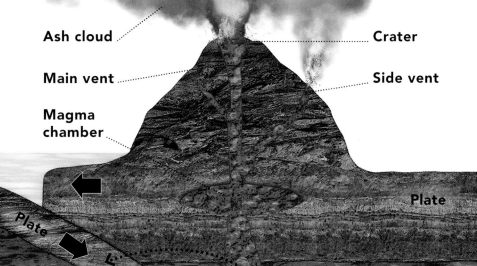

Ash cloud

Crater

Main vent

Side vent

Magma chamber

Plate

Plate

One plate pushes under another plate.

Pillow

Some volcanoes dribble lava so slowly that you can stand and watch. Others explode like bombs—*BOOM*. They can destroy an area in minutes.

A shield volcano forms when fast-flowing lava spreads over a wide area. It makes a low, gently sloping mountain.

A cinder cone volcano is made by small eruptions. Lava sprays into the air, then

Shield volcano

Cinder cone volcano

Stratovolcano

falls to make a steep slope with a crater at the top.

A stratovolcano forms quickly. It is made by big, blasting explosions. Layers of lava and ash make a steep slope with a crater at the top.

Soufrière Hills, a stratovolcano on Montserrat

Fiery god

The word *volcano* comes from Vulcan, the Roman god of fire. In myths, he lives on Mount Etna.

Mount Fuji

Stratovolcano Fuji is the highest mountain in Japan. It is worshipped as a holy place.

Pele

The Hawaiian goddess of volcanoes lives in the crater of Kilauea.

Mount Vesuvius erupts!

In the town of Pompeii, Italy, on August 24 in 79 CE, it was like night had come during the day. In the distance, the volcano Mount Vesuvius was exploding. Smoke and flames blasted high into the sky, and the air was hot and thick. Narrow streets filled with people fleeing toward the harbor. Fine ash fell from above, around the people, on them. It became harder to move. Soon they could not even breathe the poisoned air.

Some people lay down right where they were. They would never rise again.

Pliny the Younger, an eyewitness to the eruption

You might hear the shrieks of women, the screams of children, and the shouts of men; . . . some lifting their hands to the gods; but the greater part convinced that there were now no gods at all, and that the final endless night . . . had come upon the world.

THINK ABOUT IT Because of Pliny, we

Pompeii
had been
destroyed.

When the volcano erupted, the people of Pompeii had no time to get away. For many, the streets became their final resting place. Many centuries later, Pompeii

was discovered once again, buried under hardened ash. Digging down, researchers found the lost city and its people at last.

Against tourism

About 2.5 million tourists visit Pompeii every year. But Pompeii is old and fragile. All those people walking around the site take a heavy toll on the ruins.

For tourism

All those tourists spend money at Pompeii. They buy souvenirs and snacks. That money helps pay for the experts who work to look after the ruins.

Volcano heroes

In modern times, volcanologists work to predict eruptions. They want to make sure that a tragedy like Pompeii will never happen again. The scientists study volcanoes over weeks and years. Are there bulges? Are there changes in gases? Is there seismicity, or movement or shaking under the ground?

A volcanologist is at work in an ice cave...

0 1 2 3 4 5

Mount Pelée, 1902

Mount Vesuvius, 79 CE; Mount St. Helens 1980

Dr. Erik Klemetti, volcanologist

> We can capture so much more information about volcanic activity today than we could even 15 years ago.

Tiny changes may mean that magma is on the move upward. After an eruption, scientists can use the Volcanic Explosivity Index to measure its size on a scale of 0 to 8.

8

7

6

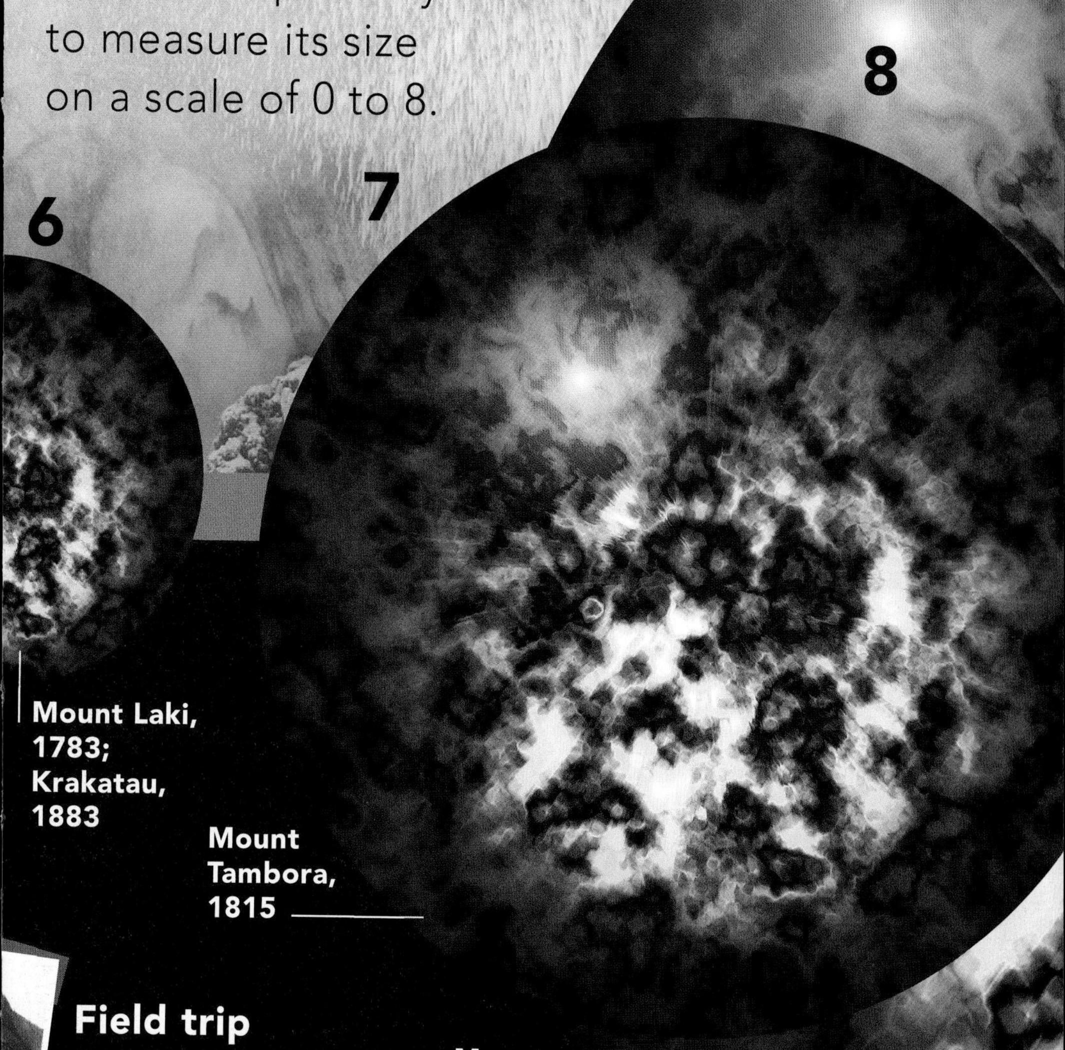

Mount Laki, 1783; Krakatau, 1883

Mount Tambora, 1815 _____

Field trip
Dr. Erik Klemetti and his students observe a Hawaiian volcano.

Mount Toba, 74,000 years ago _____

David Johnston at Mount St. Helens

One day before eruption

Mount St. Helens erupts! May 18, 1980

Volcanologists risk their lives to save others. In 1980, earthquakes had been shaking the area around Mount St. Helens, in Washington, for weeks. There had been many small eruptions. David Johnston and other scientists convinced officials to close the area to the public.

David Johnston, geologist

This is like standing next to a dynamite keg and the fuse is lit.

Mount St. Helens today

Ash, rock, and gases start to flow

Side collapses and crater grows

One month later

On May 18, a photographer was clicking away. He wanted pictures of the quiet volcano. Then, suddenly, it seemed as if half the mountain was falling down on him.

He got away, but David Johnston and 56 others were not so lucky. They died in an avalanche of lava, hot gas, and rock.

Avalanche of ash
This car was buried in ash. It was found 10 miles (16 km) from Mount St. Helens.

The Ring of Fire

Mount St. Helens is in the most explosive area on Earth. The area is called the Ring of Fire. Under the Pacific Ocean, plates move and collide. These movements made a chain

KEY

Volcanoes

Ring of Fire

Pacific ring

The Ring of Fire is 25,000 miles (40,000 km) long. It stretches from the southern tip of South America to New Zealand.

HOT FACT!

ASIA

Mount Fuji

Krakatau

Mount Tambora

AUSTRALIA

SOUTHERN OCEAN

On average, plates move as much as you

of 452 volcanoes around the ocean's edges. Underwater eruptions and earthquakes in the Ring of Fire can cause tsunamis.

NEW WORD

A **tsunami** (tsu-NAH-mee) is a giant wave that can flood a beach in minutes.

SAY IT OUT LOUD

Mount St. Helens

NORTH AMERICA

Kilauea

Mauna Loa

PACIFIC OCEAN

ingernails grow—about 1.5 in. (3.8 cm) per year.

19

The state of Hawaii sits on the Pacific plate. Hawaii's volcanoes are unusual because they are not at the edge of a plate, like most volcanoes are. They are in the middle of one!

Hawaii is on top of a volcanic hot spot. As the Pacific plate slowly moves, the hot spot spews lava. Over millions of years, layers of cooled lava built up and up. This made the first Hawaiian island.

HOT FACT!

Kilauea, a shield volcano

A hot spot is a place in Earth's mantl

Then, as the plate kept moving, the next island was formed. Island after island was created in this way.

Up on the surface, there are several volcanoes. Mauna Loa and Kilauea are the most active. They are still almost directly above the hot spot.

VOLCANO WATCHING

Hawaii

You can get close to the lava flow at Kilauea. The volcano has been erupting since 1983.

Yellowstone

Magma below Yellowstone National Park heats water underground. It shoots up through a vent as a geyser.

Crater Lake, Oregon

A caldera is a crater made when a volcano collapses. The crater may fill with water to form a lake.

...nder the plates, where magma is made.

Krakatau, in the
Ring of Fire, erupted in 1883.
It was the loudest explosion ever.
The eruption and the tsunami that
followed killed at least 36,000 people.

Even more powerful was the eruption of
nearby Mount Tambora, in 1815. Tambora's
pyroclastic flows of lava, ash, gases, and debri
killed 12,000 people right away.

A **pyroclastic** (pye-roh-KLAS-tik) flow traveled so fast down the mountain, no one in the village could escape.

Anak Krakatau erupting today

A new island

The island of Krakatau was blown apart by the blast. In 1930, a new island rose up. It had been formed by an undersea volcano.

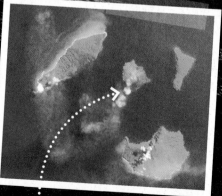

New island **Anak Krakatau is in the middle.**

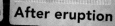

Before eruption **After eruption**

But the worst from Tambora was yet to come. By the summer of 1816, people around the world knew that something strange was happening with the weather. It was cold. Very cold.

On June 7, it snowed in the northeastern US. All that summer, every time crops looked like they might survive, frost would kill them. Earth's temperature dropped about 5 degrees that year.

The volcanic winter destroyed crops. Across the world, people and livestock starved.

Caldera
Tambora now has a caldera 3.7 miles (6 km) wide.

The cold weather was caused partly by the eruption. Ash and gases blocked the Sun's rays for many months.

April 5–17, 1815

Tambora erupts, shooting ash high into the air.

April 1815

Ash and gases begin to spread around the globe, blocking the Sun's rays.

June 7, 1816

Snow begins to fall in the northeastern US, killing crops.

June 16, 1816

In Europe, the cold and rainy weather forces Mary Shelley to stay indoors. She writes *Frankenstein*.

July 4, 1816

Fourth of July revelers bundle up in winter gear.

September 1816

Crops in the US and Europe fail. Food prices skyrocket.

1816–1819

Famine hits the US, Europe, and India. Families move west across the US in search of better land.

Volcanoes and our future

How can we keep ourselves safe from volcanoes? By studying them, scientists can warn us when an eruption might be on the way. They can help us understand how those eruptions will affect us.

Love volcanoes? Maybe you will be a volcanologist someday, making exciting new discoveries. Dangerous, destructive, yet part of the life of our planet, volcanoes will always inspire amazement and awe.

> It's amazing how something that seems permanent, like rock, comes out of the ground melted. Volcanoes have captured people's imaginations forever.
>
> Dr. Erik Klemetti, volcanologist

Awesome volcano records

Most active volcanic body

Io is one of Jupiter's moons. It has more active volcanoes than anywhere else in our solar system.

Io

Jupiter

Biggest eruption

Mount Toba, in the Ring of Fire, produced the largest volcanic eruption of the last 2 million years. It happened 74,000 years ago.

Longest recorded history

Mount Etna, in Sicily, has the longest recorded history of any volcano. The ancient Greeks wrote about it as early as 425 BCE. It is still active today.

The US' largest volcano

The caldera at Yellowstone National Park has not erupted for 600,000 years, but if it did, it could wipe out two-thirds of the US.

Old Faithful, geyser at Yellowstone

THINK ABOUT IT **You live near an**

⚠ Most deaths

The 1815 eruption of Tambora caused 92,000 deaths. Krakatau's eruption killed 36,000. Mount Pelée's eruption killed 30,000 in 1902.

⚠ Most fatal pyroclastic surge

Pyroclastic flow from Mount Pelée completely destroyed the town of Saint-Pierre, in Martinique. Almost every person in the town was killed.

⚠ Largest lava eruption

In 1783, Mount Laki, in Iceland, erupted for eight months. Crops were destroyed and livestock died. A terrible famine resulted.

Yikes! Run!

⚠ Largest volcanic tsunami

The eruption of Krakatau in 1883 caused a tsunami that was 130 feet (40 m) tall. Most of the deaths at Krakatau resulted from the tsunami.

Glossary

aa
A Hawaiian term for rough lava.

avalanche
A large amount of soil, snow, ice, or rock that suddenly falls down the side of a mountain.

bulge
An area that is swelled or sticks out.

caldera
A very large crater that can form when a volcano explodes or collapses.

cinder cone volcano
A cone-shaped volcano that is formed when debris collects around a vent.

crater
A large hole in the ground.

debris
The pieces of something that has been broken or destroyed.

dynamite
A very powerful explosive.

erupt
To suddenly throw out something, like lava and ash from a volcano.

famine
A serious lack of food in a particular area.

fragile
Easily broken.

frost
A thin layer of ice that forms on things when the weather is very cold.

geyser
An underground spring that shoots boiling water and steam into the air.

hot spot
A place where underground magma rises up to Earth's surface.

lava
The hot, liquid rock that pours out of a volcano when it erupts.

magma
Melted rock beneath Earth's surface that becomes lava when it flows out of volcanoes.

mantle
The part of Earth between the outer layer and the center.

mudflow
A moving mass of soil and water.

pahoehoe

A Hawaiian term for cooled, hard lava with a smooth surface.

permanent

Lasting for a very long time without changing.

pillow lava

Lava that cools underwater into rounded shapes like pillows.

plate

One of the large, hard, rocky pieces that make up Earth's outer layer.

predict

To guess what will happen in the future.

pyroclastic

Made up of pieces of rock from a volcano.

seismicity

The earthquake activity of an area.

shield volcano

A broad, rounded volcano that is built up by many eruptions of liquid lava.

spew

To burst out in a flood or gush.

stratovolcano

A steep volcano made up of hardened layers of ash and thick lava.

tsunami

A very large, destructive wave caused by an undersea earthquake or volcano.

vent

The opening in a volcano through which gas and lava escape.

volcanologist

A scientist who studies volcanoes.

Index

Image credits

Photography and artwork
1: Beboy_ltd/iStockphoto; 2–3t: Justin Reznick/iStockphoto; 2–3b: Keith Levit/Shutterstock; 3c: Warren Goldswain/iStockphoto; 4–5: Antonio Zanghi/Getty Images; 4bl: bubaone/iStockphoto; 6–7t: G. Brad Lewis/Science Source; 6–7 (main image): Tim Loughhead/Precision Illustration; 6br: Stephen & Donna O'Meara/Volcano Watch Int'l/Science Source; 7bl: G. Brad Lewis/Science Source; 7bc: OAR/National Undersea Research Program/Science Source; 8–9: Martin Rietze/www.mrietze.com; 8bl: Lagui/Fotolia; 8bc: Alexander Fortelny/iStockphoto; 8br: nstanev/Fotolia; 9 (globe): iStockphoto/Thinkstock; 9crt: Science Source; 9crb: prasit chansareekorn/Shutterstock; 9bc: Werner Forman/Corbis Images; 10–11 (fireballs): Jon Hughes/www.jfhdigital.com; 10 (round frame): Christopher Ewing/iStockphoto; 10–11b: Keith Levit/Shutterstock; 11 (frame): rudi wambach/iStockphoto; 11 (Pompeii): Media from the Discovery Channel's Pompeii: The Last Day, courtesy of Crew Creative, Ltd./Wikipedia; 12–13: Leonard Von Matt/Getty Images; 13cr: DHuss/iStockphoto; 13br: Christa Brunt/iStockphoto; 14–15tc: Justin Reznick/iStockphoto; 14–15 (ice cave): George Steinmetz/Corbis Images; 14–15 (lava balls): Piotr Krzeslak/Shutterstock; 14bl: Christopher Ewing/iStockphoto; 14bc, 14br: Erik Klemetti; 16–17 (t series): USGS; 16–17 (main image): USGS/CVO Photo Archive/Wikipedia; 16bl: Christopher Ewing/iStockphoto; 17br: USGS Cascades Volcano Observatory, Dan Dzurisin/AP Images; 18–19 (background): Shannon Stent/iStockphoto; 18–19 (tablet): loops7/iStockphoto; 18–19 (map): NOAA/Science Source; 18–19 (volcano graphic): Scholastic Inc.; 18–19 (Ring of Fire graphic): Andrew Robinson/iStockphoto; 20–21: Michael Szoenyi/Science Source; 21 (binoculars): Jill Fromer/iStockphoto; 21 (binocular inset): Mark Newman/Science Source; 21brt: Maridav/Fotolia; 21brc, 21brb: iStockphoto/Thinkstock; 22–23: Media Bakery; 23 (brown photo borders): Picsfive/iStockphoto; 23bl, 23bc: North Wind Picture Archives/AP Images; 23br: Landsat7 satellite, from Landsat program, NASA/Wikipedia; 24–25: NASA/Wikipedia; 25 (clock): jfelton/iStockphoto; 25r (t to b): bubaone/iStockphoto, iStockphoto/Thinkstock, browndogstudios/iStockphoto, iStockphoto/polygraphus/iStockphoto, david franklin/iStockphoto, Tomislav Forgo/iStockphoto, polygraphus/iStockphoto; 26–27 (background): Martin Rietze/www.mrietze.com; 26br: AnakaoPress/Science Source; 27tr: Christopher Ewing/iStockphoto; 28–29 (t border, volcano icons): Scholastic Inc.; 28–29 (lava): Christopher Ewing/iStockphoto; 28 (Jupiter, Io): Lars Lentz/iStockphoto; 28 (droplets, globes, penguin, bear): Scholastic Inc.; 28 (Etna): lapas77/Fotolia; 28 (flag): Sarunyu_foto/Fotolia; 28 (Old Faithful): Carlyn Iverson/Science Source; 29 (skull): polygraphus/iStockphoto; 29 (Pelée): Bettmann/Corbis Images; 29 (dog): Helle Bro Clemmensen/iStockphoto; 29 (cat): Tulay Over/iStockphoto; 29 (wave): Shannon Stent/iStockphoto; 30–31: G. Brad Lewis/SPL/Science Source; 32: Keith Levit/Shutterstock.

Cover
Front cover: (background) G. Brad Lewis/Getty Images; (cloud icon) Scholastic Inc.; (main image) Martin Rietze/Media Bakery. Back cover: (computer monitor) Manaemedia/Dreamstime. Inside front cover: bubaone/iStockphoto.

Thank you
Thank you to Dr. Erik Klemetti, for his kindness and patience in explaining many of the concepts in this book, and to Dr. Mike Goldsmith.